GRAV3YARDGIRL

PAPER DOLLS

BUNNY MEYER AND TED MENTEN

Dover Publications, Inc., Mineola, New York

C000232068

HELLO SWAMP FAMILY!

I hope that y'all will enjoy the following paper doll book. I tried to compile not only my favorite outfits, but outfits that represent some of the major milestones, events, and meet 'n greets that we as the Swamp Family have been a part of together! As always, I would like to thank each of you for your support and love. Thank you for being a part of this incredible journey with me! Without each and every one of you none of this would be possible!

HUGS & GATORS,
BUNNY

Fuzzy leopard print coat paired with a lace black top and thrifted leather pencil skirt. A favorite fall and winter outfit! Paired with UNIF 'Hellbound' platform shoes.

Silk Free People dress for my Tartelette photo shoot with Tarte, and antique metal crown. I chose this dress because of its Victorian elements. I represented the 'Free Spirit' shade in the palette.

B

B

PLATE 2

Lace leotard from Lipservice paired with a thrifted leather pencil skirt and tutu belt, and featured with one of my all-time favorites, the UNIF 'Reaper' platform shoes.

UNIF 'Detention' dress with side cutouts and UNIF 'Reaper' platform shoes.

B

B

PLATE 3

Blue and grey plaid UNIF 'Detention' dress, as featured in my "5 Spring Outfits of the Week" video in 2013. Perfect for warmer weather!

Authentic velvet-accented Victorian ensemble circa 1880. One of the outfits I am most proud of in my entire collection! I wish I could wear it every day!

B

B

PLATE 4

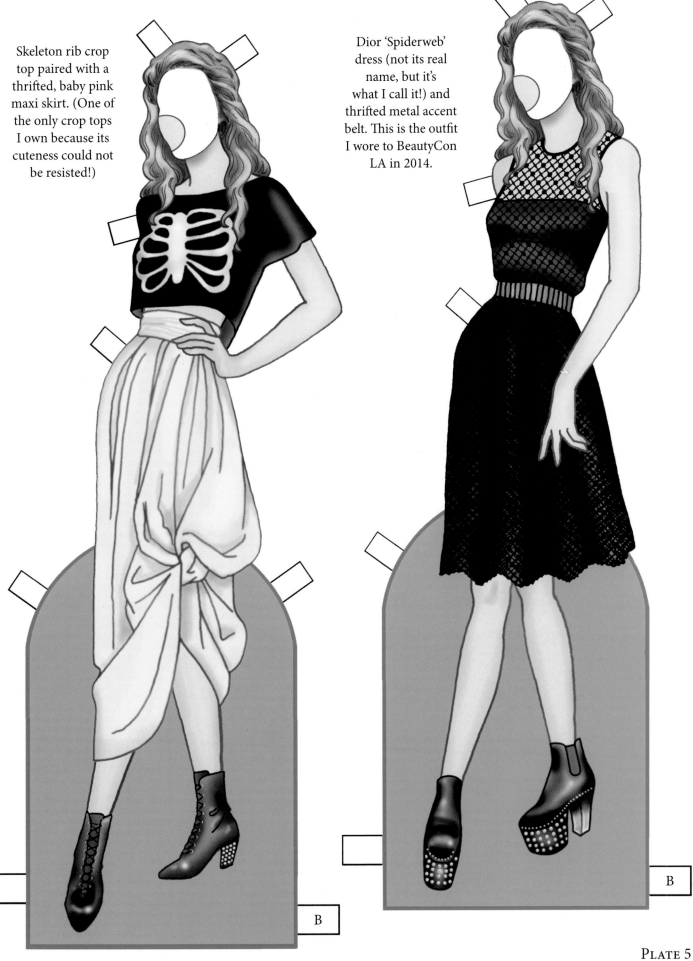

Skeleton rib crop top paired with a thrifted, baby pink maxi skirt. (One of the only crop tops I own because its cuteness could not be resisted!)

Dior 'Spiderweb' dress (not its real name, but it's what I call it!) and thrifted metal accent belt. This is the outfit I wore to BeautyCon LA in 2014.

B

B

PLATE 5

Two-piece short and jacket set from McQ by Alexander McQueen in a pale pink and houndstooth pattern. I wore this the first time I appeared on live television for a news interview in 2014.

Antique Victorian puff-sleeve jacket with lace front velvet shorts. I found this jacket in one of my favorite Austin-based clothing stores, Feathers.

Tan leather fringe jacket with sateen patterned shorts. One of my favorite 'southwestern'-themed outfits for summer!

B

B

B

PLATE 6

An outfit I wore to
my first Disneyland
meet 'n' greet in 2013.
Printed skeleton tank
top and UNIF velvet
leopard pants.

Dolce & Gabbana
wisteria-printed dress
I wore for BeautyCon
Dallas in 2015. A bit
"out of character" for
what I normally wear,
but I fell in love with
the 50s-style fit!

A

B

PLATE 7

My favorite dress to wear on Valentine's Day, a pink Betsy Johnson 'Cupcake' dress with pink Jeffrey Campbell 'Lita' boots.

One of my favorite wintertime outfits, a black blazer paired with a chunky knit sweater from Free People, and red plaid shorts.

A

A

PLATE 8

Cream cotton tank top (perfect for beating the heat in the Texas summer!) paired with knitted beige shorts.

Studded collar tank top paired with black denim shorts and a thrifted faux-fur leopard belt.

One of my most worn pieces, a leopard print tank.

PLATE 9

Black lace fit and flare skater dress and thrifted metal accent belt. I wore this outfit to IMATS in 2013.

UNIF 'Melt' maxi dress. One of my favorite summer outfits of 2014.

Do not cut out white space between arms and body.

A

A

PLATE 10

Floral bodycon
dress by Alexander
McQueen. The
first designer piece
of clothing I saved
up for and bought
myself! Very
proud to say I own
this piece.

Do not cut out
white space between
arms and body.

Betsy Johnson black
ruffle ball gown that
I wore the first time I
photographed a product
for a company. I wore
this for a Solestruck
blogger feature about the
spiked Jeffrey Campbell
'Lita' boots.

A

A

PLATE 11

My favorite type of tee—torn and tattered! I picked up this one at Wasteland, one of my favorite vintage stores in Los Angeles. It's paired with a pair of JET patchwork jeans and UNIF studded 'Reaper' platforms.

One of the clothing pieces I brought back from my first trip to Los Angeles in 2013, the UNIF 'Bad Kitty' moto jacket.

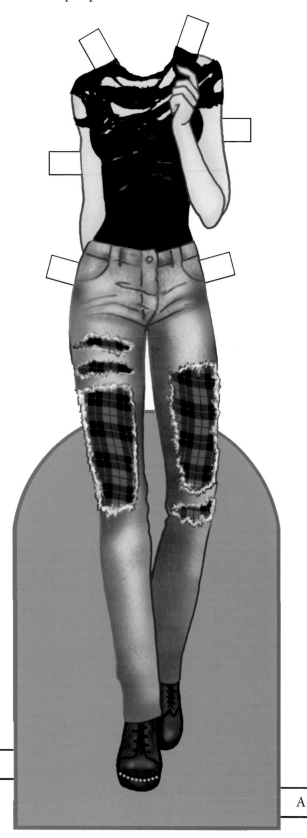

A

A comfy skull tank with scarf-front accent.

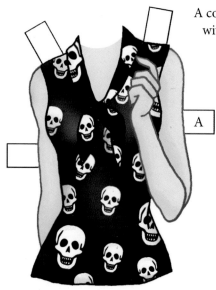

A

A

PLATE 12

The 'Nightfall' dress by Black Milk Clothing is one of my favorite "little black dresses."

Featured on my Instagram page for a "Throwback Thursday," this is the Prom dress I wore to Dogman's senior prom—A teal beadwork dress featuring a sheer mermaid bottom.

A

A

PLATE 13

Asymmetrical UNIF 'Stray' dress, paired with Substitute 'Club Kid' platforms and a chunky silver chain necklace.

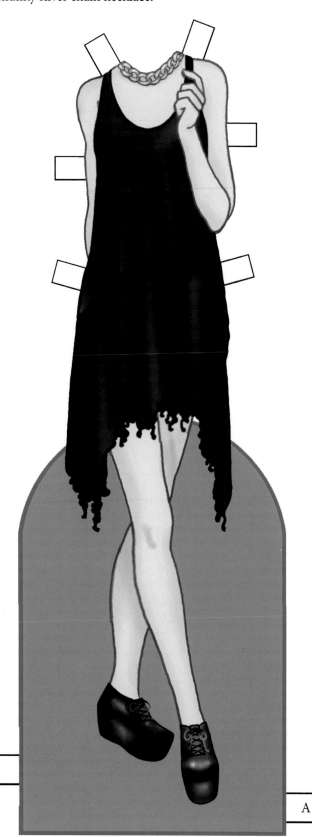

Spiked Jacket from my Dolls Kill photo shoot in San Francisco! Paired with my classic Alexander McQueen skull scarf.

Do not cut out white space between arm and body.

One of my staple wardrobe items, the UNIF 'AWOL' camo coat.

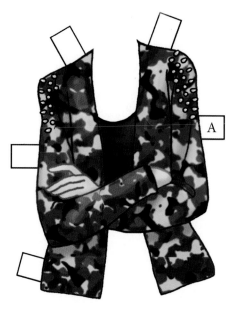

PLATE 14

This red plaid
cotton dress is
one of my casual
favorites to wear
year round!

Sequin and mesh
oversized eye dress
from Discount
Universe and studded
Prada wedges. A comfy
and casual summer
favorite!

A

A

PLATE 15

One of my favorite vintage tattered tees from Wasteland in Los Angeles, the 'Ghost of the Loco Motion', paired with asymmetrical red plaid maxi skirt and UNIF 'Hellbound' platform shoes.

'Funny Bones' leotard from Black Milk Clothing paired with a comfy cotton cage skater skirt & UNIF 'Hellbound' platform heels.

A

A

PLATE 16